THE
LAW SCHOOL
ALTERNATIVE

The shorter, more affordable
path to a law-related career

JOLENE BLACKBOURN

ISBN: 979-8-9853837-2-0

DEDICATION

For those who have goals in life but are uncertain how to fulfill them.
This book is for you.

TABLE OF CONTENTS

PREFACE

This book is meant for you if you fit into one of the following categories:

1. You want to go to law school but don't really want to be an attorney.

2. You have a good job but want something more out of it, want to reach that next level, and you're thinking some legal training is the way to do that.

3. You work with lawyers, more or less do what they do, and want to even the playing field a bit.

4. You are interested in legal-adjacent fields (Human Resources, Public Policy, Advocacy) but don't want to pay for law school.

5. You think you want to be an attorney but aren't sure you want to spend the time and money on law school.

6. You really want to be an attorney, but law school just isn't going to work out for you.

If any of those sound even remotely familiar, you **_need_** to check out this book.

Approximately 70,000 people apply to American Bar Association approved law schools every year[1]. Plenty of those who attend later regret it, so questioning the path is a smart move. The legal profession has a depression rate of approximately 30%[2]. That's not a statistic that should be taken lightly. Instead, you should do all you can to ensure you don't become part of that number.

One way to avoid joining the depressed lawyers group is to ensure law school is right for you. Understanding all your options is the best way to do that. One of those options is the Master of Legal Studies program.

Many (really, most) prospective law students have never heard of the Master of Legal Studies. There are several reasons for this. One reason is that it is a "newer" program. It is also not regulated by one organization like law schools are, so there is no centralized database to help students find it. To make matters worse, each school calls their program something different (e.g., Master of Studies in Law and Masters of Jurisprudence, just to name a few)

---

1   https://www.reuters.com/legal/legalindustry/law-school-applicants-surge-13-biggest-increase-since-dot-com-bubble-2021-08-03/

2   https://www.americanbar.org/groups/lawyer_assistance/research/colap_hazelden_lawyer_study/

so even if you try to search for a program in your area, you may not find it because the search terms are different.

To give you a quick overview of the program, an MLS (the shorthand I will use in this book) is a more or less one-year program that provides students with some legal knowledge and practical knowledge focusing on legal-adjacent areas. In many of the programs, students spend some time in law school classes with law students (although not graded against them in the vast majority of the programs), learning about contracts and other subjects that legal-adjacent careers may need to know. The students then take electives in their chosen field, such as Criminal Justice, Public Policy, or Human Resources.

Graduates cannot practice law. They simply are familiar with the law and the way that it works. However, they can work in legal fields including arbitration, mediation, and so forth. If this sounds appealing, read on!

If you are interested with respect to all things prelaw, visit https://linktr.ee/legallearningcenter so you can follow me on your favorite platform and access free stuff!

INTRODUCTION

A little background

I never really wanted to be an attorney. I went to law school because I was interested in politics, and most politicians are lawyers. Alternatively, I wanted to work in or even manage a nonprofit. You don't need to be an attorney for that, but it seemed like a good idea. In fact, I read many magazine articles that said getting a law degree was good for *anything*.

Unfortunately, that's not true. While a law degree can be helpful to working in nonlegal fields, the debt can prohibit you from taking a nonlegal job and the degree will make nonlegal employers question your motives in applying for a nonattorney job. As it turns out, companies don't read the same magazine articles prelaw students do. So legal knowledge is good. A law degree for someone interested in legal-adjacent jobs is not good.

I did go to law school. I have practiced law since that time. I have never been a politician and I have never worked for a non-profit (outside my law school internships). I lost interest in working in politics and felt I couldn't afford to work for a nonprofit after incurring so much debt.

Many years later, I began The Legal Learning Podcast to help prospective law students better understand all the things I wish I had known before I went to law school. Through a podcast guest, I learned about the MLS program.

I was fascinated. Through this guest, I was connected to Toni Jaeger-Fine of Fordham Law. Toni was gracious enough to also be a guest on the podcast to share what the MLS program is like. (If you are interested in listening to my interview of Toni Jaeger-Fine, visit: https://legallearning.libsyn.com/master-of-studies-in-law-the-jd-alternative-0)

What I learned during that interview (and in subsequent research) is that the MLS program is still somewhat of a mystery. There is really no consistent regulation of the program, which means there is no consistency in how the program is run. Honestly, it was difficult just finding the schools that offer this program because of the variety of names for the program. (For purposes of this book, we will stick with Master's of Legal Studies or MLS.)

Considering the lack of consistency, it's no wonder that college students and working professionals have never heard of the program. Many people are most likely enrolling in law school when really, a Juris Doctorate (JD) alternative would be a better fit.

This book will provide you with basic information and guidance surrounding this JD alternative. It is not meant to give you specific information. The reason I say that is because many of the websites for these programs contain very little information. I have reached out to every single school for which I could find a law school alternative program. However, some of the schools did not respond. The information shared here is therefore the most complete information I could gather with a reasonable effort. Please also keep in mind that there may be slight variations made to these programs each year so while I have every intention of updating this book, as needed, please confirm everything with any schools you are seriously considering.

Basic Requirements - Overview

To give you a general idea of what an MLS program is like, most of them require thirty units to graduate. This can be done within nine months on a full-time basis or within a few years on a part-time basis. The part-time programs typically last from two to four years, depending on how many units are taken each semester.

The subject matter covered within these programs varies greatly, as most schools allow the students to choose a specialization. The specializations can be corporate compliance, technology, healthcare, criminology, public policy, and so on.

The MLS program is generally made for working professionals. In general, this program is attractive to people who already have a career and would like to advance that career rather than change it by becoming an attorney.

One difference between the MLS programs is that some are offered at law schools and you will take classes with law students while others are treated a bit more like graduate school. Some programs that integrate MLS students with JD students keep those grading standards separate; others do not. Be sure to investigate any program you are considering so you get the experience you want.

How to use this book

In Section One, I've listed some major differences between the MLS programs and law school.

In Section Two, I've listed each of the schools by state. If you would like to attend a school near you, in person, start there.

If you are interested in a particular program, skip to Section Three. I've organized the schools by specializations offered.

If you are specifically looking to attend school online, skip to Section Four.

If you are interested only in full-time or part-time programs, I've separated them in Section Five.

Section Six is where I describe a few facts about a few special schools that may not have fit the "normal" parameters.

Section Seven is a handful of stories of MLS graduates. This program was created to help those who want law-adjacent careers.

It can be hard to know if this program is right for you. These stories should shed some light on how this program worked for them and how it may, or may not, work for you.

To help you better understand the program for yourself, I've included a handful of questions you can ask schools and graduates in Section Eight.

Finally, Section Nine was created to ensure you avoid debt as much as possible!

Disclaimer

While the following information may look straightforward, the fact that there is no one name for this program, no governing body and the names that are used for this program are extremely close to a regular master's program and the LLM (Master's of Law) program (which is a post-law school degree), it is actually very difficult to find every school that offers a law school alternative program. Add to that, the fact that a specialty could be added or dropped within months of publication, I ask for your assistance. Please let me know if you find a program that I missed. Let me know if a specialty has changed. Let me know of any discrepancy you find! This book will be updated regularly, but together, we can ensure more people get accurate information.

Also, a few programs that may have similar titles to the MLS were not included if they appeared to be more "formal," meaning they required an entrance exam (i.e., GRE, LSAT) or appeared to be more extensive than the general 30-unit programs that most MLS programs are.

Thank you!!!

SECTION ONE

Perhaps one of the biggest differences between the MLS program and other programs is that there is no entrance exam required. The application process is a lot easier than any other type of graduate level program. This has numerous benefits. No need to spend months studying for an exam. No need to spend money on the exam and study materials. No need to wait that extra time to apply. You can go now!

While every school has their own requirements, applying to an MLS program generally consists of the following:

1. A bachelor's degree
2. 1-3 letters of recommendation
3. Work experience
4. A particular GPA

5. A statement of interest
6. A standardized test of any sort (GMAT, LSAT, GRE) *may* be submitted, ***if desired***
7. Resume
8. Transcripts
9. Application
10. Personal Statement

Many schools accept applications within months of the program start date. Many schools also have ongoing enrollment, meaning you can start in August, January, and, sometimes, in other months.

Overall, it's much faster and easier to apply to an MLS program. Some schools only require one-third of the above listed information, so you could start the application process and attend your first class within weeks!

If you are already a working professional, another advantage is that the program is made for people like you. While most graduate level programs (MBA, law school, med school) exist to *create* the foundation for a career, the primary purpose of the MLS program is to *further* a career. This means that, on average, the students may be a tad older than those starting other graduate level programs. The students also tend to be a bit more focused in the sense that they are working while attending the MLS program or are attending full time with a very focused goal of getting back to work.

Law students generally don't work until months after graduation. Many times, they have to take out bar exam loans to be able to afford to live for the three months they study for the bar exam, the bar exam course, and test-related costs. All of that is avoided with the MLS program. Once you graduate, you can work. No need to wait three months for an exam and another handful of months hoping you passed.

Generally speaking, you will find little information about employment statistics from the MLS programs. Again, because this program is focused on working adults, the students do not rely as heavily on the school to find employment. There are pros and cons to this.

On the "pro" side, hopefully, you know your career path and somewhat know what you will be doing once you have your degree. Many students already have connections in their career field or have a career they are maintaining and progressing within, while they attend the MLS program.

On the "con" side, if you enter this program without any connections and little work experience and focus on an area you know nothing about prior to attending, you may not have much assistance in getting a job, in the specialty you were hoping for. If you are using the MLS program for a complete career shift, be sure to ask a lot of questions. Talk to the schools and to people who work in the field you are interested in. Make sure you are taking the right steps to reach your goal. Make sure the school can actually help you get there.

It's important to remember that this degree will not *ever* allow you to practice law, but it can take you pretty close. None of the following programs are approved by the American Bar Association, although some are acquiesced to by the ABA. This means they are acknowledged as part of the law school offerings. From my understanding, whether a program is acquiesced to or not, does not make much difference.

Finally, if you later decide you do want to go to law school, you will have to start completely over. The law schools will not give you any credit for graduating from an MLS program, although it certainly can bolster your application, and you will be better prepared than other law students.

SECTION TWO

I'd first like to list the states in which I could not find a program. If you happen to find one in one of these states, please let me know! As I said before, there are about ten different titles for this type of program making it a difficult topic to research. It's entirely possible I missed a program and would love to know if I did.

If you happen to live in a state where there is no MLS program, there are plenty of online programs so you may want to skip to Section Four.

States with no MLS programs

- Alaska
- Arkansas
- Delaware
- Hawaii

- Idaho
- Iowa
- Maine
- Mississippi
- Montana
- Nevada
- North Dakota
- South Carolina
- South Dakota
- Virginia
- Wisconsin
- Wyoming
- Guam
- Puerto Rico

States that have law school alternative programs

- Alabama
  - Samford University - Cumberland School of Law

- Arizona
  - Arizona State University - Sandra Day O'Connor College of Law
  - The University of Arizona - James E. Rogers College of Law

- California
  - Abraham Lincoln University
  - California Southern University
  - Loyola Law School
  - Pepperdine University - Caruso School of Law
  - Santa Barbara College of Law
  - Santa Clara University School of Law
  - Stanford Law School
  - University of California Hastings Law
  - University of California, Los Angeles School of Law
  - University of San Diego School of Law
  - University of Southern California - Gould School of Law
  - University of the Pacific - McGeorge School of Law
  - Ventura College of Law

- Colorado
  - Sturm College of Law - University of Denver
  - University of Colorado Boulder - Colorado Law

- Connecticut
  - University of New Haven
  - Yale Law School

- Florida
  - Florida International University College of Law

- Florida State University College of Law

- Georgia
  - Emory University School of Law
  - University of Georgia School of Law

- Illinois
  - DePaul University - College of Law
  - Loyola University Chicago - School of Law
  - Northwestern University - Pritzker School of Law
  - University of Illinois - College of Law
  - University of Illinois - Springfield

- Indiana
  - Purdue University Global

- Kansas
  - Washburn University School of Law

- Kentucky
  - Northern Kentucky University

- Louisiana
  - Loyola University New Orleans - College of Law
  - University of Louisiana at Monroe

- Maryland
    - University of Maryland - Francis King Carey School of Law

- Massachusetts
    - Northeastern University School of Law
    - Regent University School of Law
    - Suffolk Law School

- Michigan
    - Wayne State University Law School

- Minnesota
    - Hamline University
    - University of St. Thomas School of Law

- Missouri
    - Washington University in St. Louis School of Law
    - Webster University

- Nebraska
    - University of Nebraska - Lincoln

- New Hampshire
    - University of New Hampshire - Franklin Pierce School of Law

- New Jersey
  - Seton Hall Law School

- New Mexico
  - New Mexico State University
  - University of New Mexico School of Law

- New York
  - Albany Law School
  - Cornell Law School
  - Fordham University Law School
  - Hofstra Law
  - New York University School of Law
  - Yeshiva University - Cardozo School of Law

- North Carolina
  - Wake Forest School of Law

- Ohio
  - Capital University Law School
  - Case Western Reserve University School of Law
  - Cleveland - Marshall College of Law
  - The Ohio State University - Moritz College of Law
  - University of Akron School of Law

- Oklahoma
  - Oklahoma City University School of Law
  - The University of Oklahoma College of Law

- Oregon
  - Lewis & Clark Law

- Pennsylvania
  - California University of Pennsylvania
  - Drexel University - Thomas R. Kleine School of Law
  - The Pennsylvania State University - Dickinson Law
  - University of Pittsburgh School of Law

- Rhode Island
  - Roger Williams University School of Law

- Tennessee
  - University of Tennessee Knoxville College of Law

- Texas
  - St. Mary's School of Law
  - Texas A&M University School of Law

- Utah
  - The University of Utah - S.J. Quinney College of Law

- Vermont
  - Vermont Law and Graduate School

- Washington
  - Seattle University School of Law

- West Virginia
  - American Public University
  - West Virginia University

- Washington, D.C.
  - American University Washington College of Law
  - George Washington Law
  - Georgetown University Law Center

**A few programs were terminated or put on hold in the last few years. This includes Iowa Law, UIC John Marshall Law School, Michigan State University College of Law and Western Connecticut State University. You may want to check back later if you are interested in these schools.

SECTION THREE

The specializations offered at law school alternative programs have been organized by *broad* topics. When you specifically research your schools of interest, the exact name of the specialization may differ slightly. For example, one school may offer a Dispute Resolution focus while another might offer an Arbitration, Mediation and Negotiation focus. These are listed together, as they are somewhat similar topics.

Keep in mind that many schools do not offer specializations. If you do not see your preferred school as one that offers your particular topic, be sure to investigate what electives they offer. The school may still have several electives in that field without specifically offering it as a "specialization."

Areas of focus

- Administrative Law
  - Florida State University College of Law
  - The Pennsylvania State University - Dickinson Law

- Admiralty and Maritime Law
  - Roger Williams University School of Law

- Applied Research
  - Purdue University Global

- Arbitration, Mediation, Negotiation/Dispute Resolution
  - Arizona State University - Sandra Day O'Connor College of Law
  - Hamline University
  - Pepperdine University - Caruso School of Law
  - Regent University School of Law
  - Roger Williams University School of Law
  - The Ohio State University - Moritz College of Law
  - The Pennsylvania State University - Dickinson Law
  - University of California Hastings Law
  - University of California, Los Angeles School of Law
  - Washington University in St. Louis School of Law

- Banking
  - Florida International University College of Law

- Biomedical and Health Services Research
  - University of Pittsburgh School of Law

- Biotechnology Business/genetics/molecular biology
  - Suffolk Law School

- Business/Business Administration and Marketing
  - Abraham Lincoln University
  - American University Washington College of Law
  - Arizona State University - Sandra Day O'Connor College of Law
  - DePaul University - College of Law
  - Emory University School of Law
  - Florida State University College of Law
  - George Washington Law
  - Loyola Law School
  - Northeastern University School of Law
  - Northern Kentucky University
  - Northwestern University - Pritzker School of Law
  - Regent University School of Law
  - Roger Williams University School of Law
  - Santa Barbara College of Law
  - St. Mary's School of Law

- ○ Texas A&M University School of Law
- ○ The Pennsylvania State University - Dickinson Law
- ○ University of California Hastings Law
- ○ University of California, Los Angeles School of Law
- ○ University of Pittsburgh School of Law
- ○ University of San Diego School of Law
- ○ University of Southern California - Gould School of Law
- ○ University of Tennessee Knoxville College of Law
- ○ Ventura College of Law
- ○ Wake Forest School of Law
- ○ Washburn University School of Law
- ○ Washington University in St. Louis School of Law

- • Commercial Law
  - ○ St. Mary's School of Law
  - ○ University of Pittsburgh School of Law

- • Compliance and Enterprise Risk Management
  - ○ Case Western Reserve University School of Law
  - ○ Florida State University College of Law
  - ○ Loyola University Chicago - School of Law
  - ○ Seattle University School of Law
  - ○ St. Mary's School of Law
  - ○ Texas A&M University School of Law
  - ○ The University of Arizona - James E. Rogers College

of Law

- ○ University of California Hastings Law
- ○ University of Southern California - Gould School of Law
- ○ Washington University in St. Louis School of Law

- Comprehensive Examination
  - ○ Purdue University Global

- Constitutional Law
  - ○ George Washington Law
  - ○ Roger Williams University School of Law
  - ○ The Pennsylvania State University - Dickinson Law

- Construction Law
  - ○ Arizona State University - Sandra Day O'Connor College of Law
  - ○ Texas A&M University School of Law

- Contracts
  - ○ Arizona State University - Sandra Day O'Connor College of Law
  - ○ Florida State University College of Law
  - ○ University of Tennessee Knoxville College of Law

- Corporate Compliance
  - Arizona State University - Sandra Day O'Connor College of Law
  - Fordham University Law School
  - Oklahoma City University School of Law
  - Santa Clara University School of Law
  - The Ohio State University - Moritz College of Law
  - University of Pittsburgh School of Law

- Criminal Justice/Law/Procedure
  - Abraham Lincoln University
  - Arizona State University - Sandra Day O'Connor College of Law
  - California University of Pennsylvania
  - Capital University Law School
  - DePaul University - College of Law
  - Drexel University - Thomas R. Kleine School of Law
  - Florida State University College of Law
  - George Washington Law
  - Loyola Law School
  - New Mexico State University
  - Northern Kentucky University
  - Regent University School of Law
  - Roger Williams University School of Law
  - St. Mary's School of Law
  - The Ohio State University - Moritz College of Law

- ○ The Pennsylvania State University - Dickinson Law
- ○ The University of Arizona - James E. Rogers College of Law
- ○ University of California Hastings Law
- ○ University of Louisiana at Monroe
- ○ University of New Hampshire - Franklin Pierce School of Law
- ○ University of Pittsburgh School of Law
- ○ University of San Diego School of Law
- ○ University of Tennessee Knoxville College of Law
- ○ Washburn University School of Law
- ○ West Virginia University

- Crisis Management Law
  - ○ University of Maryland Francis King Carey School of Law

- Cybersecurity and Data Privacy
  - ○ Albany Law School
  - ○ Cleveland - Marshall College of Law
  - ○ Drexel University - Thomas R. Kleine School of Law
  - ○ Florida State University College of Law
  - ○ George Washington Law
  - ○ Loyola Law School
  - ○ Regent University School of Law
  - ○ Roger Williams University School of Law

- Seton Hall Law School
- Suffolk Law School
- Texas A&M University School of Law
- The Pennsylvania State University - Dickinson Law
- University of Maryland - Francis King Carey School of Law
- Yeshiva University - Cardozo School of Law

- Disability Law
  - University of Pittsburgh School of Law

- Education Law
  - Florida International University College of Law
  - Hamline University
  - St. Mary's School of Law

- Elder Law
  - University of Pittsburgh School of Law

- Emerging Law
  - Santa Barbara College of Law
  - Ventura College of Law

- Entertainment and Media Law
  - Loyola Law School
  - University of California, Los Angeles School of Law

- ○ University of Pittsburgh School of Law
- ○ University of Southern California - Gould School of Law

- Environmental and Energy/Water/Natural Resources
  - ○ Arizona State University - Sandra Day O'Connor College of Law
  - ○ Capital University Law School
  - ○ Florida State University College of Law
  - ○ George Washington Law
  - ○ Lewis and Clark Law School
  - ○ Roger Williams University School of Law
  - ○ St. Mary's School of Law
  - ○ Sturm College of Law - University of Denver
  - ○ Texas A&M University School of Law
  - ○ The University of Arizona - James E. Rogers College of Law
  - ○ The University of Oklahoma College of Law
  - ○ University of California Hastings Law
  - ○ University of California, Los Angeles School of Law
  - ○ University of Georgia School of Law
  - ○ University of Maryland Francis King Carey School of Law
  - ○ University of New Mexico School of Law
  - ○ University of Pittsburgh School of Law
  - ○ University of San Diego School of Law

- University of Tennessee Knoxville College of Law
- University of the Pacific - McGeorge School of Law
- Vermont Law and Graduate School
- Washburn University School of Law

- Estate Planning
  - University of Pittsburgh School of Law
  - Washburn University School of Law

- Ethics and Compliance
  - University of Colorado Boulder - Colorado Law
  - University of St. Thomas School of Law

- Family and Juvenile/Children's Law
  - Loyola University Chicago - School of Law
  - Roger Williams University School of Law
  - The University of Arizona - James E. Rogers College of Law
  - University of Pittsburgh School of Law
  - Washburn University School of Law

- Financial Services Compliance
  - Albany Law School
  - Case Western Reserve University School of Law
  - Drexel University - Thomas R. Kleine School of Law
  - Florida State University College of Law

- ○ George Washington Law
- ○ Seton Hall Law School
- ○ University of California Hastings Law

- Food and Agriculture
  - ○ Vermont Law and Graduate School of

- Government
  - ○ Capital University Law School
  - ○ George Washington Law
  - ○ Oklahoma City University School of Law
  - ○ The Pennsylvania State University - Dickinson Law
  - ○ University of California Hastings Law
  - ○ University of California, Los Angeles School of Law
  - ○ University of Tennessee Knoxville College of Law
  - ○ University of the Pacific - McGeorge School of Law
  - ○ Washburn University School of Law

- Health Care
  - ○ Albany Law School
  - ○ American University Washington College of Law
  - ○ Arizona State University - Sandra Day O'Connor College of Law
  - ○ Capital University Law School
  - ○ DePaul University - College of Law
  - ○ Drexel University - Thomas R. Kleine School of Law

- Emory University School of Law
- Florida International University College of Law
- Florida State University College of Law
- George Washington Law
- Hofstra Law
- Loyola University Chicago - School of Law
- Loyola University New Orleans - College of Law
- Northeastern University School of Law
- Regent University School of Law
- Seattle University School of Law
- Seton Hall Law School
- St. Mary's School of Law
- Texas A&M University School of Law
- The Pennsylvania State University - Dickinson Law
- The University of Arizona - James E. Rogers College of Law
- The University of Oklahoma College of Law
- University of California Hastings Law
- University of California, Los Angeles School of Law
- University of Georgia School of Law
- University of Maryland - Francis King Carey School of Law
- University of Pittsburgh School of Law
- University of Southern California - Gould School of Law
- University of Tennessee Knoxville College of Law

- ○ Wake Forest School of Law
- ○ West Virginia University

- Higher Education Compliance
  - ○ Drexel University - Thomas R. Kleine School of Law

- Homeland/National Security and Military Law
  - ○ California University of Pennsylvania
  - ○ Regent University School of Law
  - ○ Roger Williams University School of Law
  - ○ St. Mary's School of Law
  - ○ University of California, Los Angeles School of Law
  - ○ West Virginia University

- Human Resources and Employment Law/Labor Law
  - ○ Arizona State University - Sandra Day O'Connor College of Law
  - ○ Capital University Law School
  - ○ Drexel University - Thomas R. Kleine School of Law
  - ○ Florida State University College of Law
  - ○ Northeastern University School of Law
  - ○ Northern Kentucky University
  - ○ Pepperdine University - Caruso School of Law
  - ○ Regent University School of Law
  - ○ Roger Williams University School of Law
  - ○ Texas A&M University School of Law

- ○ The Ohio State University - Moritz College of Law
- ○ University of California Hastings Law
- ○ University of California, Los Angeles School of Law
- ○ University of Georgia School of Law
- ○ University of Pittsburgh School of Law
- ○ University of Southern California - Gould School of Law
- ○ University of Tennessee Knoxville College of Law
- ○ University of the Pacific - McGeorge School of Law
- ○ Wake Forest School of Law
- ○ Washington University in St. Louis School of Law
- ○ Wayne State University Law School

- Immigration
  - ○ Regent University School of Law
  - ○ Roger Williams University School of Law
  - ○ University of California Hastings Law

- Indian/Indigenous People Law
  - ○ Arizona State University - Sandra Day O'Connor College of Law
  - ○ The University of Arizona - James E. Rogers College of Law
  - ○ The University of Oklahoma College of Law
  - ○ University of New Mexico School of Law

- Intellectual Property
  - Arizona State University - Sandra Day O'Connor College of Law
  - Case Western Reserve University School of Law
  - George Washington Law
  - Northeastern University School of Law
  - Northern Kentucky University
  - Northwestern University - Pritzker School of Law
  - Roger Williams University School of Law
  - Seton Hall Law School
  - Suffolk Law School
  - Texas A&M University School of Law
  - The Ohio State University - Moritz College of Law
  - The Pennsylvania State University - Dickinson Law
  - The University of Arizona - James E. Rogers College of Law
  - University of California Hastings Law
  - University of Georgia School of Law
  - University of New Hampshire - Franklin Pierce School of Law
  - University of Pittsburgh School of Law
  - University of San Diego School of Law

- International Law
  - Arizona State University - Sandra Day O'Connor College of Law

- ○ DePaul University - College of Law
- ○ Roger Williams University School of Law
- ○ St. Mary's School of Law
- ○ The Ohio State University - Moritz College of Law
- ○ University of California Hastings Law
- ○ University of San Diego School of Law

- International Trade and Business Law
  - ○ Regent University School of Law
  - ○ Texas A&M University School of Law
  - ○ The University of Arizona - James E. Rogers College of Law
  - ○ The University of Oklahoma College of Law

- International Trial Advocacy
  - ○ The Pennsylvania State University - Dickinson Law

- Legal Administration
  - ○ Sturm College of Law - University of Denver

- Litigation, Trial Advocacy and Legal Process
  - ○ Hamline University
  - ○ Pepperdine University - Caruso School of Law
  - ○ Roger Williams University School of Law
  - ○ The Pennsylvania State University - Dickinson Law
  - ○ University of California Hastings Law

- ○ University of California, Los Angeles School of Law
- ○ Washington University in St. Louis School of Law

- Media and Publishing
  - ○ Northern Kentucky University

- Mining Law and Policy
  - ○ The University of Arizona - James E. Rogers College of Law

- Pharmaceutical and Medical Device Law and Compliance
  - ○ Drexel University - Thomas R. Kleine School of Law
  - ○ Seton Hall Law School

- Professional Practice Management
  - ○ Hamline University

- Public Administration
  - ○ University of New Haven

- Public Interest Law/Nonprofit
  - ○ DePaul University - College of Law
  - ○ Regent University School of Law
  - ○ The Pennsylvania State University - Dickinson Law
  - ○ University of California, Los Angeles School of Law

- Public Policy
    - California University of Pennsylvania
    - Emory University School of Law
    - Iowa Law
    - Northeastern University School of Law
    - University of Georgia School of Law
    - University of Illinois - Springfield
    - University of New Hampshire - Franklin Pierce School of Law
    - University of the Pacific - McGeorge School of Law

- Real Estate Law/Land Use Law
    - Roger Williams University School of Law
    - Texas A&M University School of Law
    - University of Pittsburgh School of Law

- Regulatory Compliance
    - Regent University School of Law
    - Suffolk Law School
    - University of Illinois - Springfield

- Restorative Justice
    - University of New Hampshire - Franklin Pierce School of Law
    - Vermont Law and Graduate School

- Rule of Law for Development
  - Loyola University Chicago - School of Law

- Social Justice/Human Rights
  - Hamline University
  - The Pennsylvania State University - Dickinson Law
  - University of California Hastings Law
  - University of Colorado Boulder - Colorado Law
  - University of Illinois - Springfield
  - University of Pittsburgh School of Law
  - University of Tennessee Knoxville College of Law

- Sports Law
  - Arizona State University - Sandra Day O'Connor College of Law
  - Drexel University - Thomas R. Kleine School of Law
  - Loyola Law School
  - University of Pittsburgh School of Law

- Start-ups and Entrepreneurship
  - Arizona State University - Sandra Day O'Connor College of Law
  - Santa Barbara College of Law
  - Seattle University School of Law
  - St. Mary's School of Law
  - University of California Hastings Law

- ○ University of Pittsburgh School of Law
- ○ Ventura College of Law

- • Tax
  - ○ DePaul University - College of Law
  - ○ Georgetown University Law Center
  - ○ New York University School of Law
  - ○ Roger Williams University School of Law
  - ○ St. Mary's School of Law
  - ○ Sturm College of Law - University of Denver
  - ○ The Pennsylvania State University - Dickinson Law
  - ○ The University of Arizona - James E. Rogers College of Law
  - ○ University of California Hastings Law
  - ○ University of Pittsburgh School of Law
  - ○ University of San Diego School of Law
  - ○ Washburn University School of Law
  - ○ Washington University in St. Louis School of Law

- • Technology
  - ○ American University Washington College of Law
  - ○ Arizona State University - Sandra Day O'Connor College of Law
  - ○ Santa Barbara College of Law
  - ○ Seattle University School of Law
  - ○ Texas A&M University School of Law

- ○ The Ohio State University - Moritz College of Law
- ○ University of California, Los Angeles School of Law
- ○ Ventura College of Law

- Territorial Law
  - ○ St. Mary's School of Law

- Wealth Management
  - ○ Texas A&M University School of Law

SECTION FOUR

M ost schools have an online component or are completely online. Some programs have online restrictions, such as you needing to occasionally show up or some of their "majors" are not available to online students. The best way to use this section is, if you are interested in an online program and a particular area of study, go to Section Three, check out which schools offer the subjects you are interested in. Then, come back here to see if they offer an online program. If they do, be sure to call them to see what the restrictions are before you waste any more of your time planning to attend any particular school.

The following schools offer online programs:

- Abraham Lincoln University
- Albany Law School
- American Public University

- Arizona State University - Sandra Day O'Connor College of Law
- California University of Pennsylvania
- Cleveland - Marshall College of Law
- Cornell Law school
- DePaul University - College of Law
- Drexel University - Thomas R. Kleine School of Law
- Emory University School of Law
- Florida State University College of Law
- Fordham University Law School
- George Washington Law
- Georgetown University Law Center
- Hamline University
- Hofstra Law
- Lewis and Clark Law School
- Loyola University Chicago - School of Law
- Loyola University New Orleans - College of Law
- New Mexico State University
- New York University School of Law
- Northeastern University School of Law
- Northern Kentucky University
- Northwestern University - Pritzker School of Law
- Oklahoma City University School of Law
- Pepperdine University - Caruso School of Law
- Purdue University Global
- Regent University School of Law

- Samford University - Cumberland School of Law
- Santa Barbara College of Law
- Seattle University School of Law
- Seton Hall Law School
- Sturm College of Law/University of Denver
- Texas A&M University School of Law
- The Ohio State University - Moritz College of Law
- The Pennsylvania State University - Dickinson Law
- The University of Arizona - James E. Rogers College of Law
- The University of Oklahoma College of Law
- The University of Utah - S.J. Quinney College of Law
- University of California, Los Angeles School of Law
- University of Illinois - Springfield
- University of Louisiana at Monroe
- University of Maryland Francis King Carey School of Law
- University of New Hampshire - Franklin Pierce School of Law
- University of New Haven
- University of Southern California - Gould School of Law
- University of St. Thomas School of Law
- University of Tennessee Knoxville College of Law
- University of the Pacific - McGeorge School of Law
- Ventura College of Law
- Vermont Law and Graduate School
- Wake Forest School of Law

- Washington University in St. Louis School of Law
- Wayne State University Law School
- Webster University
- West Virginia University
- Yeshiva University - Cardozo School of Law

SECTION FIVE

The minimum time needed to complete this program is nine months. For part-time programs, students typically attend for two years. However, many schools allow up to four years to complete the program. The record holder is eight years! So, there is a lot of flexibility at some of these schools.

In addition to full-time vs. part-time programs, I've listed the number of units required by the school to complete the program and the school's timeframe for completing those units.

You will notice that some information doesn't quite add up. For example, some schools say they offer both full- and part-time programs but then say the program is one year. I'm sure you can do the math on that. So, consider this a general guideline! Again, that is because many of the schools were not responsive and I could not find this information on their website.

Full-time only

- Albany Law School (30 units) (1 year)
- California Southern University (36 units) (2 years)
- Florida International University College of Law (30 units) (1 year)
- Washington University in St. Louis School of Law (24 units) (1 year)

Both full-time and part-time programs offered

- Abraham Lincoln University (30 units) (5 semesters)
- American Public University (36 units) (1+ years)
- American University Washington College of Law (30 units) (12+ months)
- Arizona State University - Sandra Day O'Connor College of Law (30 units) (1 year+)
- California University of Pennsylvania (30 units) (1 - 2 years)
- Capital University Law School (30 units) (1 - 4 years)
- Case Western Reserve University School of Law (30 units) (9 - 18 months)
- Cleveland - Marshall College of Law (30 units) (20 months - 5 years)
- DePaul University - College of Law (30 units) (1.5 - 6 years)

- Drexel University - Thomas R. Kleine School of Law (30 units)
- Emory University School of Law (30 units) (9 months - 4 years)
- Fordham University Law School (30 units) (1 year)
- George Washtington Law (24 units) (1+ years)
- Georgetown University Law Center (24 units) (1 - 5 years)
- Hamline University (34 units) (18+ months)
- Hamline University (34 units) (18+ months)
- Lewis and Clark Law School (26 units) (9 months - 3 years)
- Loyola Law School (24 units) (18 months)
- Loyola University New Orleans - College of Law (30 units) (1 year - 3 years)
- New Mexico State University (33 units) (2 - 3 years)
- Northeastern University School of Law (30 units) (1 year - 1.5 years)
- Northern Kentucky University (30 units) (1 year - 3 years)
- Northwestern University - Pritzker School of Law (28 units) (9 months - 4 years)
- Pepperdine University - Caruso School of Law (32 units) (16 months - 3 years)
- Purdue University Global (55 units) (1 year)
- Regent University School of Law (30 units) (1 year+)
- Roger Williams University School of Law (30 units)
- Santa Barbara College of Law (30 units)
- Santa Clara University School of Law (36 units) (1 - 2 years)
- Seattle University School of Law (30 units) (1 - 2 years)
- St. Mary's School of Law (30 units) (9 months - 3 years)

- Sturm College of Law/University of Denver (30 units) (9 months - 2.5 years)
- Suffolk Law School (30 units) (9+ months)
- Texas A&M University School of Law (30 units) (1 - 2 years)
- The Ohio State University - Moritz College of Law (30 units) (9 months - 2 years)
- The Pennsylvania State University - Dickinson Law (24 units) (9 months)
- The University of Arizona - James E. Rogers College of Law (30 units) (1- 4 years)
- University of Akron School of Law (30 units) (1+ years)
- University of California Hastings Law (24 units) (1.5 - 4 years)
- University of California, Los Angeles School of Law (26 units) (9 months - 4 years)
- University of California, Los Angeles School of Law (26 units) (9 months - 4 years)
- University of Colorado Boulder - Colorado Law (28 units) (9 months - 2.5 years)
- University of Georgia School of Law (30 units) (1 - 3 years)
- University of Illinois - College of Law (32 units) (1 - 2 years)
- University of Louisiana at Monroe (30 units) (18 months - 3 years)
- University of Nebraska - Lincoln (33 units) (1 - 3 years)
- University of New Hampshire - Franklin Pierce School of Law (30 units) (1 - 5 years)
- University of New Mexico School of Law (30 units) (1 - 4 years)

- University of Oklahoma College of Law (32 units) (15 months - 5 years)
- University of Pittsburgh School of Law (30 units) (9 months - 4 years)
- University of San Diego School of Law (26 units) (1 - 4 years)
- University of Southern California - Gould School of Law (21 units) (2 - 9 semesters)
- University of Tennessee Knoxville College of Law (30 units) (1 - 4 years)
- Ventura College of Law (30 units)
- Vermont Law and Graduate School (30 units) (1 - 5 years)
- Washburn University School of Law (30 units) (1 - 4 years)
- Wayne State University Law School College of Law (30 units) (within 6 years)
- Webster University (39 units)
- West Virginia University (30 units) (18 months - 8 years)
- Yeshiva University - Cardozo School of Law (30 units) (2+ years)

Part-time only

- Cornell Law School (30 units) (20 months)
- Florida State University College of Law
- Hofstra Law (30 units) (2 - 5 years)
- Loyola University Chicago - School of Law (24 units) (2 years)
- New York University School of Law (24 - 30 units) (3 - 5 years)
- Oklahoma City University School of Law (2 years+)

- Samford University - Cumberland School of Law (34 units) (2 years)
- Seton Hall Law School (31 units) (2 years)
- University of Illinois - Springfield (36 units) (2 years)
- University of Maryland - Francis King Carey School of Law (30 units) (2 years)
- University of New Haven (36 units)
- University of St. Thomas School of Law (30 units) (21 months)
- University of the Pacific - McGeorge School of Law (26 units) (2 years)
- Wake Forest School of Law (30 units) (21 months - 5 years)

SECTION SIX

This section of the book is for a few special notes on a few special schools.

Yale

Their school almost didn't qualify for this book because they require that students already have a doctoral degree before attending the MLS program! But, if your undergraduate degree was in journalism, you get a pass, and can proceed directly to their MLS program. To be clear, do not apply for Yale's MLS program unless your undergraduate degree was in journalism. Their program requires 27 units in 9 months.

Concord Law School

Concord offers a unique program that doesn't quite fit in here, but I wanted to mention it. They offer an EJD, an Executive Juris Doctor. It is a three-year, online program that will earn you a doctorate (if you are having trouble letting go of that title) but still won't make you a lawyer. It will give you the same legal knowledge and training that the MLS program will, but over three years. Seventy-two units are required. Credit is given to students who first obtain their MLS from Purdue University Global.

Some schools offer dual degree programs. Their MLS can be combined with a JD, PhD, MD, or other program. A joint degree could be a great fit if you want to pursue the medical field but better understand the law or want to be an attorney but would like some "practical" knowledge as well (something like a focus on entrepreneurship or management to help you run your law firm).

SECTION SEVEN

These are stories of real students. The good, the bad, and the ugly. These stories should give you a better idea of who can benefit from this type of program and in what way. This program will not be the right fit for everyone. It's important to evaluate this in light of your own circumstances. These stories should help you with that.

If you want to hear more stories or share your own, please contact/follow me on Instagram at https://www.instagram.com/legal-learningcenter/. I would love to share your MLS story on my page!

KJ's story

KJ took ten gap years before applying for law school. She was working as a flight attendant and felt unprepared to return to school. Her mom suggested the MLS program as a way to prepare herself for law school. KJ applied about a week before fall classes started. She was accepted, quit her job, and started school all in about one week!

Her program was technically meant to be completed in a year and a half. KJ still intended to enroll in law school the following year, so she completed it in just one.

While every program is different, there were people in her program who had enrolled in law school the prior year but did not have the grades to stay. This particular program allowed those ex-law students to apply some of the law school units from their 1L year to the MLS program.

One of the things KJ really liked about her program was the ability to take classes with law students who were in their second and third year of school. She specifically chose the school she attended because she was an entrepreneur, and her school had an entrepreneurial focus.

She also liked that MLS students were not graded on a curve like the law students were, so there was no competition between students. Even in the classes with law students, they were not in competition with them. So, MLS students could help each other and the law students and actually make friends and connections.

For KJ, the MLS program helped her be better prepared for 1L year. She knew how to write an exam, the basic legal lingo and how law school worked. The program also solidified her conviction that law school was the right path for her.

She also feels that having a master's degree has been helpful in her job search. It has often been a topic of discussion in interviews and enabled her to participate in an entrepreneurial program at her law school, a year earlier than she would have otherwise been able to. At her law school, the entrepreneurial program is only open to 2L and 3L students. She was able to participate in the program during her 1L year. Again, this gave her an advantage when looking for internships and jobs.

Tom's story

Tom had a career working in regulatory compliance auditing for an insurance company. A few years ago, he needed back surgery and wanted to use that down time productively and possibly make a career change, so he enrolled in an MLS program. He knew he didn't want to be an attorney. He also didn't want the extensive loans that come with law school. There are plenty of jobs that seek "JD preferred" candidates. Tom planned to attend the MLS program and seek a "JD preferred" position.

At Tom's school, most students were in their mid-to-late twenties. Many were looking to move up in their career, rather than make a career change. Despite thirteen gap years, Tom did not feel the program was overly demanding.

It's only been a few months since Tom graduated from the MLS program and he is still working at his original job while seeking new employment. He has not received a raise for attending the MLS program or graduating.

Overall, Tom recommends that you know what you want before you start. He liked the MLS program and recommends it to anyone who wants to work in the legal field but doesn't want to be an attorney.

Vanessa's story

In 2018, Vanessa was a paralegal, working in-house in the legal department of a global retail company. She had been a paralegal for about five years and felt stuck. Law school seemed too expensive and it wasn't really what she wanted. She wanted to further her career, not become an attorney. She found an MLS program that provided a focus in fashion. Considering her job was already in retail/fashion, this seemed to be a good fit.

Vanessa planned to maintain her job and attend school part time. Unfortunately, she discovered her job, with its long hours, would not accommodate her personal goals. She left that company and worked for an insurance company in their corporate compliance department. After one year as an employee, the insurance company paid for a good portion of her tuition!

Vanessa started her MLS degree in 2019 and graduated in 2021. She also shifted her focus to corporate compliance and ethics.

Vanessa felt the support system at her school was fantastic. Students were paired with a "buddy" who was either a more advanced MLS student or a JD student. JD students were in her classes, although they were not graded against them. Her program had about 35 students. She felt that the staff, students, and adjunct professors were helpful toward her career. She even obtained her current job, in corporate compliance, through a colleague at school.

Vanessa loved her program and feels she obtained the exact benefit she was hoping to gain from it. She noticed her classmates did as well. Overall, she recommends this program for those wanting to further their career and not for those who just want to use it as a warm-up for law school. Her friend went to law school at the same time she attended this program, and she believes adding another year on to law school is too much and can wear you down.

Samantha's story

Samantha was working full time for the Department of Justice and part-time for Amazon when she became inspired to attend an online MLS program. While still working for those jobs, she attended school, focusing on criminal law (based on her current job), business law (to further her bachelor's degree), and contract management law.

Samantha took five gap years before starting her MLS journey. She worked full-time and attended school at night and on weekends, also on a full-time basis. She chose her particular school because it was the cheapest of the online programs. Some other programs cost as much as $60,000!

While Samantha's GPA in undergrad was not the best, her MLS program loved her personal statement, and she was accepted immediately. Her grades in the MLS program were much higher than in college. She felt more focused and interested in the MLS classes. They were also offered in an eight-week format, rather than semester-long. This enabled her to focus more specifically on each topic.

Samantha had a few goals for her future. She was interested in possibly creating concert venues, furthering her positioning within her current job or becoming an investigator. With the areas of focus offered by her school, she could make any of the paths a reality.

Samantha did not want to be an attorney. She didn't want the loans or the stress. With the MLS program, Samantha learned how to write case briefs and read court opinions. She wrote papers that she is now using as writing samples for job applications. She found her professors made themselves available to the students. She liked the way her school was organized and felt there were many resources available to the students.

Samantha thinks the MLS program is great if you want to get your law degree but are hesitant to pursue it. This program can help get your feet wet so you can see if you want to pursue law further.

Samantha graduated just over a year ago. She is still working her pre-graduation job. They did not give her a raise for her new degree, but the government (again the DoJ) does not necessarily give raises that way anyway. She is, therefore, seeking her raise by applying to new positions, as well as seeking external employment in law-related fields.

SECTION EIGHT

To ensure you get what you want out of this program, here are a few questions you should ask any school you are considering as well as a few questions you should ask graduates from that school. Hint: Don't use the graduates the school recommends. Instead, find them on LinkedIn. In general, it's easiest to get a response from someone who has a shared connection so if you are struggling with this, you are more than welcome to connect with me and hopefully find someone in my network (I have over 10,000, so hopefully, there will be someone!).

School

1. Will I be taking classes with law students?
   a- Which classes?
   b- How does that work?

2. What is the atmosphere like between students?

   a- Is it competitive?

   b- Are there networking opportunities between students?

   c- Are there organizations/clubs/etc?

3. Is my area of focus offered online/in person?

4. Are there networking opportunities with potential employers?

5. What employment opportunities are available? (Note: It appears most schools don't have much of a department for this as many students are already working.)

6. Is there anything I can do careerwise, before attending, to ensure I reach my career goals post graduation?

Graduates who work in your ideal career

1. Do you feel the MLS program helped you with your career goals?

2. Do you have any suggestions for things I should do before starting the program to ensure I reach my goals?

3. Do you have any suggestions for things I should do during the program to ensure I reach my goals?

4. Is there another path that will help me reach my goals?

5. Any words of warning, things to look out for?

SECTION NINE

Even though the MLS programs are only one year, they still cost a lot of money! They seem to average around $30,000. When you add in student loan interest, that turns out to be closer to $45,000. In fact, if you take out $30,000 in loans at 5% interest, you will pay $8000 in interest for a 10 year loan and $18,000 in interest for a 20 year loan!

To calculate the amount of interest you will pay if you finance your student loans, visit https://legallearningcenter.com/calculator/

Now let's talk about how to avoid this debt load.

I've come up with five ways to avoid student loan debt.

Method One

Pay cash. How hard is this? Not that hard. But also, not always possible. Let me walk you through what it might look like.

The average college student starting salary is over $50,000.[1] That means the monthly salary is $4,000. Could you save $1,000 a month? This is something I was able to do while living at home with my dad and making only $24,000 (a million years ago). Meagan, the very first guest on my podcast, The Legal Learning Podcast, was able to save $1,000 a month, while making around $35,000 a year and not living at home.[2]

Based on the stories of myself and Meagan, if you're making $50,000, you should be able to save $2,000 a month. Please note, I'm not saying this is possible for everyone. I know some of you have children or other reasons you need every dollar! However, using the aforementioned figures, it would take you 30 months (just over 2 years) to pay cash for school at $1,000 a month and only 15 months if you could actually save $2,000 a month.

Could you get a side job to bring in that extra money? Could you sell or rent out things that you own? Every little bit helps. Even paying for half of the program is exponentially better than funding the entire thing through loans.

And remember, by paying $30,000 in cash, you are actually saving $40,000 or more! It's well worth the effort.

---

1   https://www.cnbc.com/2021/09/01/college-graduate-starting-salaries-are-at-an-all-time-high.html

2   The Legal Learning Podcast - Episode 1 - Leaving the Law After 1L Year

Method Two

Talk to the school. Some have their own scholarships or offer discounts if you attend their full-time program. For example, at USC you can save as much as $14,000 simply by attending full time. So definitely check out this difference with any school you are looking into! And at The University of New Haven, correctional officers get 50% off tuition! Be sure to ask any school you apply to for any similar type of discounts!

Method Three

Some employers will pay for this program. Ask your employer!

Method Four

Compare loans. Not all loans are created equal. I recommend, whether you are taking out private or federal loans, that you compare any offers against Juno. Juno can often offer rates lower than the federal government. They do this by negotiating with lenders in bulk. You will be placed in a group of similar students, enrolling in similar programs, with similar credit scores. The lenders then offer Juno a better rate because they are doing bulk business.

These are private loans. There are benefits to federal loans (such as the fact that they are eliminated if you die before repaying them) so be sure to talk to a financial advisor to ensure any offer from Juno is better for *you* in the long run.

If you do use Juno, I'd appreciate it if you signed up through my link. It is an affiliate program in which they thank me for introducing you to them, at no cost to you. Just browse over to joinjuno.com/p/legallearningcenter for more information.

Method Five

Let's talk about third party scholarships. Ashley Hill is a scholarship search strategist and founder of Scholarship Success School.[3] She suggests you can maximize your chances of getting scholarships by focusing on local, smaller ones and by creating your own personal brand. The more you know what's unique about you, the better you can convey that message and successfully obtain those scholarships!

She recommends you first create a roadmap so you can more easily see which scholarships you are aiming for and which are a bad fit. Start first with you. Create a profile. What do you know about you? What is unique about you? Once you have a solid list of personal and professional qualities and experiences, then look at the scholarships. This should help you sift through them more quickly.

---

3   The Legal Learning Podcast - Episode 36 - Scholarships for Law School

She recommends two further tips for success. First, be consistent. If you consistently apply, you're going to get the scholarships. Second, if you aren't getting any scholarships, look at yourself. Maybe you need more volunteer work, or you need to expand your network.

If you need help with any of this, Scholarship Success School offers DIY help and DFY (Done For You) help so be sure to check them out!

After the fact

Okay, so you had to take out some loans. Here's what I recommend. Pay them off as fast as possible. The faster you pay off the debt, the less interest you will pay and the less you will pay overall. So, push through just a little longer. With your (hopefully) increased salary post graduation, I hope you can put at least $2,000 a month toward the loans so you can pay off any amount within a year or so.

CONCLUSION

It can be really hard to know whether law school is the best option for you or not. No one can give you a final answer on that. Most likely, even you cannot give yourself that answer with any real level of certainty. Even people who claim they know that the only thing they want out of life is to be an attorney, sometimes later regret it. So don't ever think that you're the only one full of doubt and insecurities.

Attending an MLS program before law school may cost you a lot more money, but it may also help you know what you really want.

Attending an MLS program when you wanted to attend law school but could not make that happen due to your at-home circumstances, may be a lifesaver!

And attending a MLS program instead of law school when all you really wanted was a bit of legal knowledge to help with your career plans, could save you tens, even hundreds of thousands of dollars.

Remember that everyone is on a different path. What is right for your friend or someone you follow on Instagram is not necessarily right for you. In fact, I interviewed several people on The Legal Learning Podcast who either dropped out of law school or left law fairly quickly in their career, specifically because I wanted prelaw students to know that life does not always turn out the way we expect, and that's OK! Just because we say we are going to do something (like go to law school), doesn't mean we *have* to. And at any point, if we change our mind, it's OK!

Don't waste hundreds of thousands of dollars pursuing a career that you're not positive you want to do. Law school will be there. Take your time. Have fun. Enjoy life. Pursue other interests, both personally and professionally. Consider other ways to pursue your dreams and then decide. And just know, even not making a decision, is making a decision.

If you want to read more about all things law school and preparing for law school, be sure to get a copy of *The Pre-Law Survival Guide,* available on Amazon.com and soon, your university bookstore!

I wish you all the best in your legal journey!

ACKNOWLEDGMENTS

I'd like to thank Megan Smiley who graciously agreed to be a guest on The Legal Learning Podcast. She shared her life's learning moments so openly and made a vital and totally random reference to the MLS program.

I'd like to further thank her for introducing me to Toni Jaeger-Fine, assistant dean at Fordham Law School, which leads me to a big thank you to Toni for taking the time to come on The Legal Learning Podcast and answer all my questions about their MLS program. Without Toni, I'd still be wandering around clueless! Thanks ladies!

Finally, I'd also like to thank Samantha, KJ, Vanessa, and Tom for sharing their MLS experiences with me. I wish you guys the best of luck in your careers!

ABOUT THE AUTHOR

Jolene Blackbourn, Esq. is a first-gen, California Estate Planning Attorney who spent way too much money on law school, considering she never wanted to be an attorney. She was a prime candidate for the MLS programs, had they ex-isted so long ago. This is her third book helping prospective law students. She has plans for several more!

When not writing, Jolene enjoys playing soccer, archery, all things Halloween, spending time with her four children (two human, two canine), and exploring California.

CAN YOU HELP?

Thank You For Reading My Book!

I really appreciate all of your feedback, and I love hearing what you have to say.

Please leave me an honest review on Amazon, letting me know what you thought of the book.

This helps me spread the word and helps me help more students!

Thanks so much and best wishes for your legal journey!

Jolene Blackbourn, Esq.

www.ingramcontent.com/pod-product-compliance
Lightning Source LLC
Chambersburg PA
CBHW060254150626
46553CB00019BA/2297